D1480737

# JUSTIN BIEBER

POP STAR

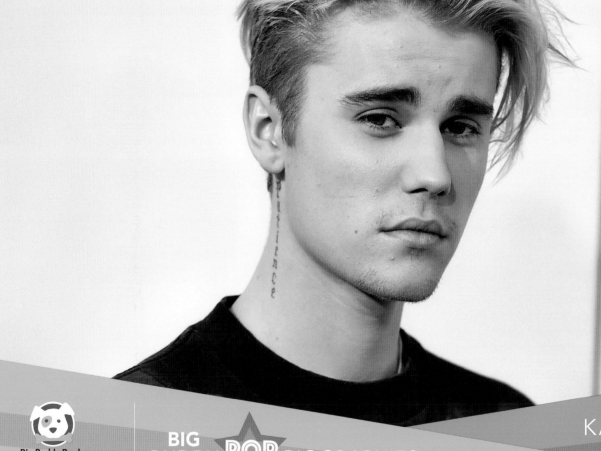

KATIE LAJINESS

Big Buddy Books
An Imprint of Abdo Publishing
abdopublishing.com

BIG BUDDY POP BIOGRAPHIES

**abdopublishing.com**

Published by Abdo Publishing, a division of ABDO, PO Box 398166, Minneapolis, Minnesota 55439.
Copyright © 2018 by Abdo Consulting Group, Inc. International copyrights reserved in all countries.
No part of this book may be reproduced in any form without written permission from the publisher.
Big Buddy Books™ is a trademark and logo of Abdo Publishing.

Printed in the United States of America, North Mankato, Minnesota.
052017
092017

THIS BOOK CONTAINS
RECYCLED MATERIALS

Cover Photo: Jordan Strauss/Invision/AP.
Interior Photos: AF archive/Alamy Stock Photo (p. 23); ASSOCIATED PRESS (pp. 11, 13, 17, 25, 27);
    dpa picture alliance/Alamy Stock Photo (pp. 5, 15); Entertainment Pictures/Alamy Stock Photo
    (p. 23); Eric Charbonneau/Invision/AP (p. 6); Jack Fordyce/Shutterstock.com (p. 29); REUTERS/
    Alamy Stock Photo (p. 11); Stephen Barnes/Alamy Stock Photo (p. 15); The Photo Access/
    Alamy Stock Photo (p. 21); WENN Ltd/Alamy Stock Photo (p. 9); ZUMA Press, Inc./Alamy Stock
    Photo (19).

Coordinating Series Editor: Tamara L. Britton
Graphic Design: Jenny Christensen

Publisher's Cataloging-in-Publication Data

Names: Lajiness, Katie, author.
Title: Justin Bieber / by Katie Lajiness.
Description: Minneapolis, MN : Abdo Publishing, 2018. | Series: Big buddy
    pop biographies | Includes bibliographical references and index.
Identifiers: LCCN 2016962359 | ISBN 9781532110597 (lib. bdg.) |
    ISBN 9781680788440 (ebook)
Subjects: LCSH: Bieber, Justin, 1994- --Juvenile literature. | Singers--Canada
    --Biography--Juvenile literature.
Classification: DDC 782.42164092  [B]--dc23
LC record available at http://lccn.loc.gov/2016962359

# CONTENTS

# POP STAR

Justin Bieber is a **pop** singer. His popular songs and albums top the music charts. Fans watch him on TV and read about him in magazines. Millions of fans on **social media** love to keep up with what he's doing!

## SNAPSHOT

**NAME:**
Justin Drew Bieber

**BIRTHDAY:**
March 1, 1994

**BIRTHPLACE:**
London, Ontario, Canada

**POPULAR ALBUMS:**
*My World 2.0, Believe,
Journals, Purpose*

# FAMILY TIES

Justin Drew Bieber was born in London, Ontario, Canada, on March 1, 1994. His parents are Jeremy Bieber and Pattie Mallette.

Justin's parents separated when he was ten months old. His mother raised him in Stratford, Ontario. Growing up, Justin saw his dad regularly.

Justin attended the 2015 *Justin Bieber's Believe* movie premiere with his mother (*second from right*) and grandparents.

# WHERE IN THE WORLD?

CANADA

QUEBEC

ONTARIO

Vermont

London

Michigan

New York

UNITED STATES

Ohio

Pennsylvania

ATLANTIC OCEAN

N
W E
S

# EARLY YEARS

Early on, Justin was a gifted **performer**. At age 12, he placed second in a talent show called Stratford Star. To showcase his skills, Justin's mom posted videos on a website called YouTube.

A music **producer** saw Justin's videos. Then, he asked Justin to **audition**. At age 14, Justin signed a recording contract.

Justin and his mom traveled to Atlanta, Georgia, for his audition.

# RISING STAR

From the beginning, fans couldn't get enough of Justin's music. In 2009, he **released** his first single, "One Time." Justin had four hit singles before his first album *My World* came out. The album sold more than 1 million copies.

In 2011, Justin went to Indonesia to give a concert.

During his concerts, Justin often brings fans on stage.

Fans followed Justin on **social media** and watched him on TV. They wanted to know the latest news about his music and **performances**.

From 2009 to 2011, Justin put out three albums. In 2012, Justin **released** *Believe*. His song "Boyfriend" had a new sound that helped him gain more fans.

12

In 2012, Justin performed at the MuchMusic Video Awards in Toronto, Canada.

# BIEBER FEVER

Justin continued to find new ways to charm his fans. In 2013, he **released** a new song every week for ten weeks. Later, these songs were part of an album called *Journals*.

Fans loved Justin's music. Three of his songs reached number one on the Billboard Hot 100 chart. They stayed on the chart for up to 41 weeks.

Justin's fans are known as Beliebers.

Fans show their love for Justin by making heart shapes with their hands.

# SOCIAL MEDIA SENSATION

Justin is a **social media** sensation. He has more than 91 million followers on Twitter. His videos on YouTube have been watched more than 14 billion times!

Fans enjoy chatting about Justin's music and his personal life. They love when he posts new photos.

Over the years, Justin has taken many pictures with fans. Oftentimes, these photos are posted on social media.

# BIG COMEBACK

Over the years, Justin has struggled with his fame. He made some poor decisions and got into trouble. Some fans felt like Justin let them down. So, he worked hard to gain their respect again. And, many people are positive Justin will continue to succeed.

During a 2015 interview, Justin said he forgot how much he loved being on stage and performing for a crowd.

Justin's more **mature** sound helped him gain new fans. His 2015 album was called *Purpose*. Each single was number one on the Billboard 100 chart.

In 2016, he received eight Guinness World Records. One record was, "What Do You Mean?" was listened to more than 30.7 million times in one week.

Justin's hit singles from *Purpose* were "What Do You Mean?," "Love Yourself," and "Sorry."

# SCREEN TIME

Justin is often funny on TV. He made people laugh on *Saturday Night Live*. And, Justin has **performed** and been **interviewed** on *The Ellen Degeneres Show*.

He has also appeared on *The Late Late Show with James Corden*. Justin and James had fun singing **pop** songs while driving in a car.

Justin has been in two documentary movies. These movies show him behind the scenes on his concert tours.

23

# AWARD SHOWS

Justin is no stranger to **award** shows. He has been **nominated** for seven **Grammy Awards**. And, he has won one. Justin has taken home five major **Teen Choice Awards**. Fans love to see Justin **perform** at these shows.

**DID YOU KNOW** ?

Justin worked with producers Skrillex and Diplo on "Where Are Ü Now." This song won a Grammy Award in 2015.

In 2015, Justin traveled to Milan, Italy, for the MTV Europe Music Awards. There, he won five awards.

# GIVING BACK

Giving back is important to Justin. He went to Guatemala with a group called Pencils of Promise. There, Justin helped build a school. He later made a video about the experience.

Justin also helped some fans in Oklahoma. Their homes were ruined in a storm. Justin wanted them to feel better. So, he gave them tickets to one of his concerts.

Justin went home to Canada for a good cause. Money from this 2015 show went to a food shelf in his hometown.

# BUZZ

Justin's fame continues to grow. And, his songs shoot to the top of the music charts. Justin often travels around the world to give concerts. He is always coming up with new and exciting ways to **perform**. Fans are excited to see what's next for Justin.

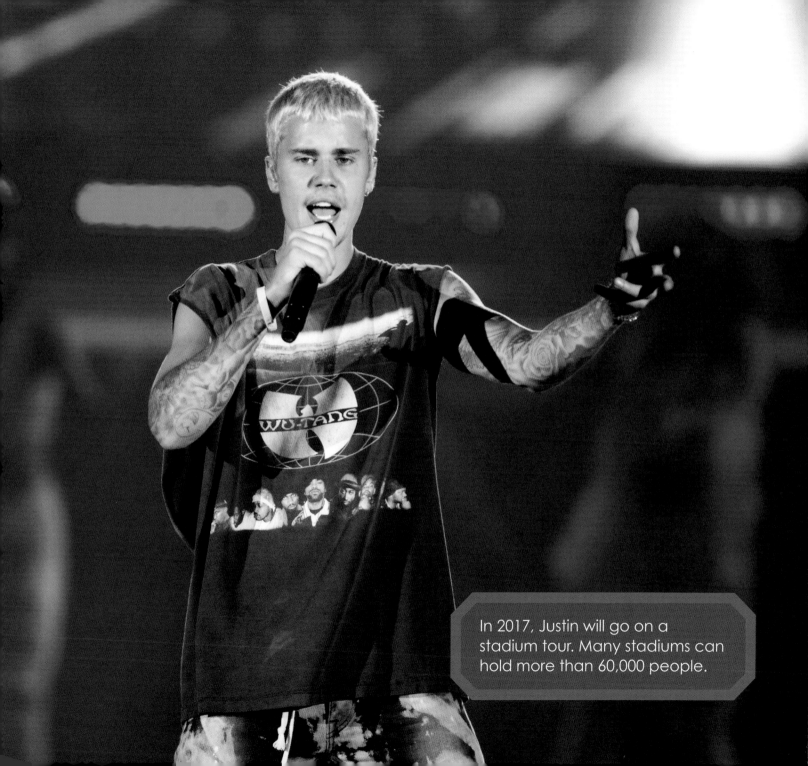

In 2017, Justin will go on a stadium tour. Many stadiums can hold more than 60,000 people.

# GLOSSARY

**audition** (aw-DIH-shuhn)  to give a trial performance showcasing personal talent as a musician, a singer, a dancer, or an actor.

**award**  something that is given in recognition of good work or a good act.

**Grammy Award**  any of the awards given each year by the National Academy of Recording Arts and Sciences. Grammy Awards honor the year's best accomplishments in music.

**interview**  to ask someone a series of questions.

**mature**  having completed natural growth and development.

**nominate**  to name as a possible winner.

**perform**  to do something in front of an audience. A performer is someone who performs. A performance is the act of doing something, such as singing or acting, in front of an audience.

**pop**  relating to popular music.

**producer** a person who oversees the making of a movie, a play, an album, or a radio or television show.

**released** to make available to the public.

**social media** a form of communication on the Internet where people can share information, messages, and videos. It may include blogs and online groups.

**Teen Choice Awards** any of the awards given each year by fans who vote online. Teen Choice Awards honor those in the entertainment and athletic industries.

# WEBSITES

To learn more about Pop Biographies, visit **abdobooklinks.com**. These links are routinely monitored and updated to provide the most current information available.

# INDEX